Purr More, Hiss Less

Heavenly Lessons I Learned from My Cat

By Allia Zobel Nolan
Illustrations by Erika Oller

Health Communications, Inc.
Deerfield Beach, Florida

www.hcibooks.com

Library of Congress Cataloging-in-Publication Data

Zobel-Nolan, Allia.
    Purr more, hiss less : heavenly lessons I learned from my cat / Allia Zobel Nolan;
illustrations by Erika Oller.
      p. cm.
    ISBN-13: 978-0-7573-0638-9 (trade paper)
    ISBN-10: 0-7573-0638-1 (trade paper)
    1. Cats—Humor. 2. Conduct of life—Humor. I. Title.
PN6231.C23Z69 2007
818'.5402—dc22

2007041644

© 2008 Allia Zobel Nolan
Illustrations © 2008 Erika Oller

HCI, its logos and marks are trademarks of Health Communications, Inc.

Publisher: Health Communications, Inc.
          3201 SW 15th Street
          Deerfield Beach, FL 33442

Cover and inside book design by Andrea Perrine

Dedication

For God; my husband, Desmond; my dear friend, Sheila; and of course, the puddies, Angela, McDuff, and Sinead, who, with more purrs than hisses, have made my life heavenly.

—AZN

In memory of Bean, very much loved and missed.

—EO

Introduction

I have always said that my precious felines were more angel than mammal. Anyone who has ever really known or loved a cat would likely agree. You need only look into their humongous eyes to find love that has no conditions (other than shrimp twice a month and a nanny who lives in), and to observe an unfailing selflessness with which they share headless mice and decomposed chipmunk remains. As I watch my beloved felines go about their lives in a manner befitting only the most righteous of beings, they have convinced me, on numerous occasions, that they must have come straight from above.

Okay, so I have no documented proof that my cats are angels. But if, indeed, you can tell a book by its cover and a person by his actions, then, surely, you can take the metal of a cat by the virtues she teaches.

I've learned many lessons from my gossamer-haired cherub, Angela, as well as from her sibling spirits, McDuff and Sinead. They've taught me by example how not to hold grudges (spit, hiss, and get over it), the importance of sharing (never bring dead snakes home unless you have enough for everyone), and how to be content in any situation (as long as you have a warm lap to lie in).

This book celebrates that feline wisdom, as well as other important life lessons I've gleaned from the other cat angels I've been blessed to have had in my life over the years. Enjoy it, and remember to keep attuned to your own cat's behavior: You never know. She could be teaching you something heavenly, too.

—Allia Zobel Nolan

You can never rub up against a person's leg too often.

If at first you don't succeed, take a nap and try again.

Happiness doesn't depend on how many milk bowls you have.

Don't be a show-off.

Strive for balance.

16

If you can't say anything nice about mice, don't say anything at all.

Love your enemies.

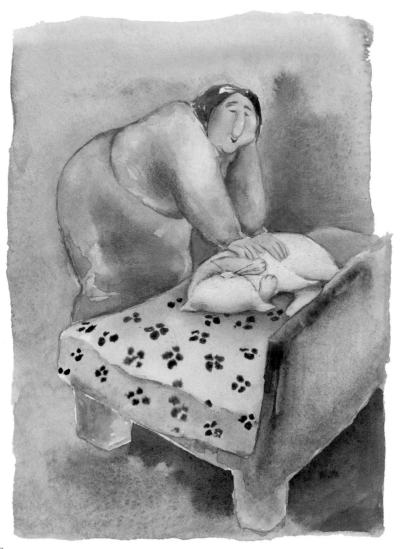

Be vulnerable.

If you must give in to anger, hiss, spit,
then get over it.

You're one of a kind–

so don't be a copycat.

It's okay to be hooked on a feline.

Don't worry; be silly.

Sit in the sun every chance you get.

31

Avoid negative thinking.

Give freely, without expecting
anything in return.

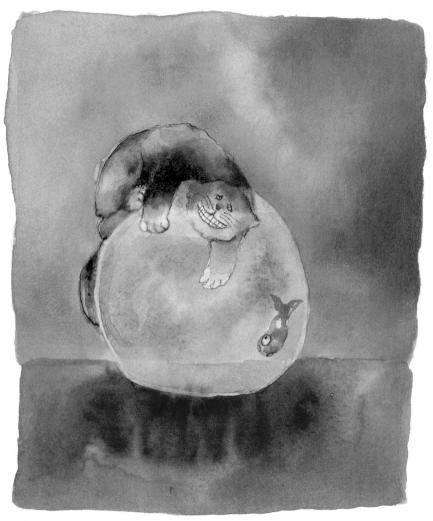

Don't be embarrassed to own up to your mistakes.

All things in moderation . . .

except toys.

40

Don't be afraid to trust.

Fighting takes away from the time you could be chasing butterflies.

If someone needs a mouse, give of your storehouse freely.

It's better to use your head
than your claws.

It doesn't matter what
color you are, or whether you're
short-haired or long-haired.

Stargaze often.

You can sleep anywhere if
you have a clear conscience.

Be happy for your neighbor's
accomplishments.

Never stick your tongue out
at visitors.

Avoid gluttony . . . unless
it's absolutely necessary.

Be inconspicuous.

If someone tries to engage you in a catfight . . . walk away.

Delight in the simple pleasures.

Offer a shoulder for friends
to lean on.

Do the right thing . . . even when there's no one watching.

Make a joyful noise!

Think before you pounce.

If you must walk all over people,

do it quickly.

Live in the moment.

Differences are what
make us interesting.

Hear no evil;

see no evil;

speak no evil.

It's okay to follow, but
never lead anyone on.

Don't cry over spilt milk.

It's more fun to chase mice
than success.

Be flexible.

It's better to lie around
than to lie.

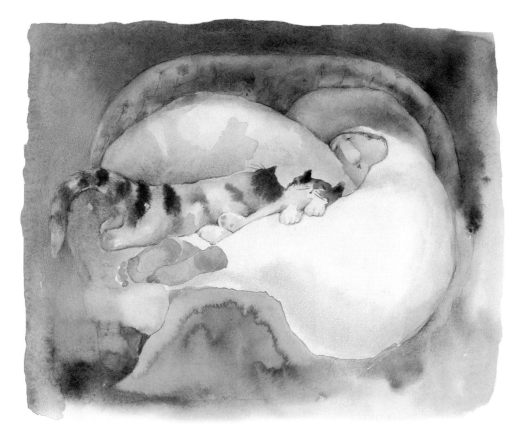

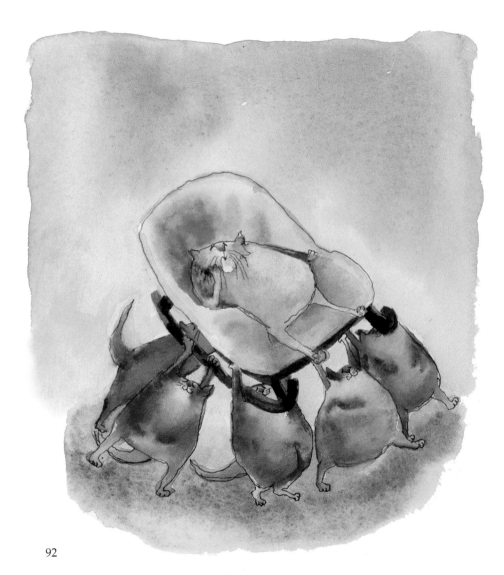

Good friends are worth more
than a truck full of shrimp.

Purr more; hiss less.

Count your blessings.

Give to those less fortunate.

You can't hold a grudge
and play with a catnip toy.

Don't stick your paws where
they don't belong.

Surprise the people you love.

Avoid being catty.

If someone steps on your tail,
forgive and forget.

Be a good listener.

Bird watching defuses stress.

You can find heaven on earth.

Don't be embarrassed to accept help from others.

Embrace change.

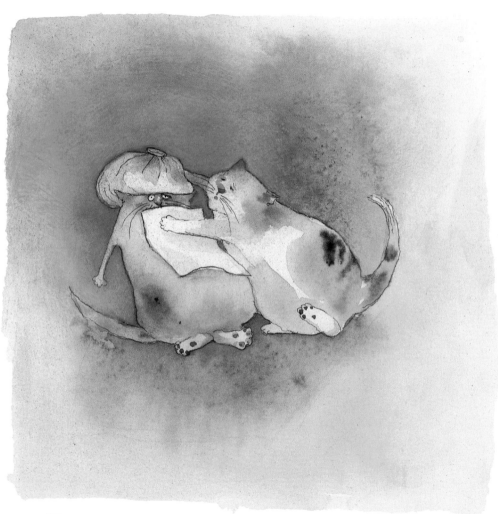

Be kind to those
with allergies.

Never beg for attention.

124

Stay on top of things.

Resist the temptation to judge others.

128

Seek and ye shall find.

Happiness is contagious.

Pass it on!

If someone's having a

bad hair day,

be sympathetic.

God doesn't care
how much you weigh.

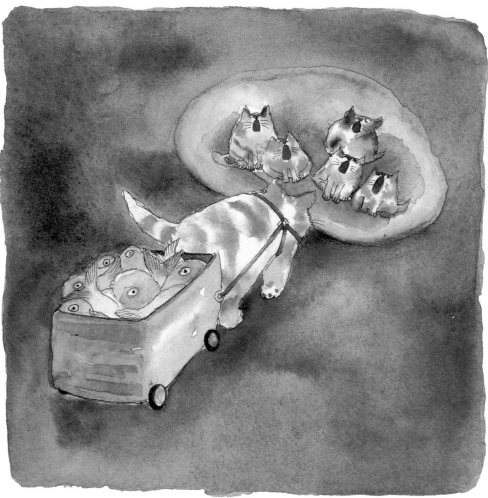

Share your good fortune.

Resist the urge to claw
your way to the top.

You win over more people with a purr than a hiss.

Smell everything.

144

Retain a kitten-like sense of wonder.

Don't be a slave to
your possessions.

You can never say
"I love you" too much.

149

Be open to criticism.

It is better to give
than to receive.

Life is precious,

even if you have

nine of them.

155

156

You don't need a corner office; a sunny windowsill should suffice.

158

You're better off with
a warm lap than a laptop.

God doesn't care what
kind of house you live in
or whether your collar
is plain or fancy.

Rejoice and be glad!

Relax without guilt.

Don't be greedy.

Grow old gracefully.

170

Cleanliness is next to godliness.

Never covet your neighbor's
cat carrier.

173

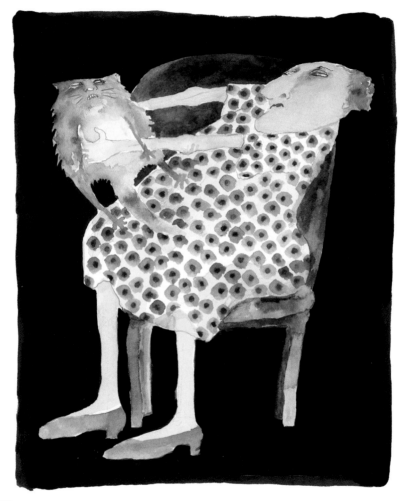

174

Flatulence is a fact of life.

If you're polydactyl . . . celebrate! God loves you that way.

177

It's okay to be "kneedy."

Don't walk away from gossips . . . run!

Avoid provocative clothing.

Sing more; whine less.

Be your brother's keeper.

Unconditional love is the best love.

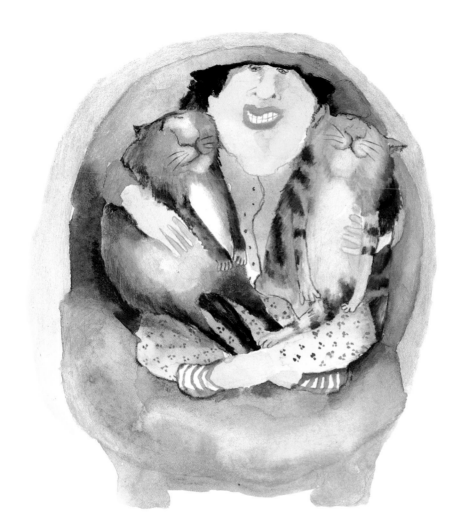

189

Patience is a virtue.

191

Visit the sick.

Take time to stare out the window.

Stretching soothes the soul.

Accept your neighbor for who he is.

199

200

Do not worship idols.

Learn to respect
the opinion of others.

Seize the day.

Enjoy quiet times with friends.

208

Be true to yourself.

Celebrate family resemblances.

Treat yourself to
something special now and again.

It's okay to stumble
on the ladder of success.

Remember, home is where the heart is.

Take the good fleas
with the bad.

Be nice to strangers.

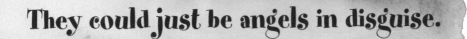

They could just be angels in disguise.

About the Author

*A*llia Zobel Nolan is an internationally published author of over 140 books, with more than two-and-a half-million books in print, including the classic *101 Reasons Why a Cat Is Better Than a Man*, the recently published *202 Reasons Why a Cat Is Better Than a Man*, and *Women Who Love Cats Too Much*. Her humor articles about cats have been featured in *Cosmopolitan* and *Glamour*. She purrs more and hisses less in Connecticut, where she lives and works with her husband, Desmond, and her puddies, Angela, McDuff, and Sinead.

About the Illustrator

*E*rika Oller is an internationally known watercolorist, who has had numerous exhibits in the United States, France, and England. Oller's artwork can be seen on calendars, several million greeting cards, adult and children's books, including *The Cabbage Soup Solution; Cats, Cats, Cats!; The Dog Who Sang at the Opera,* and more. She is represent-

ed by the Esther Wells Collection in Laguna Beach, California, and Touchstone Gallery in Yachats, Oregon. Her licensed work features everything from dinnerware to apparel and stationery. She studied at the National Academy of Design, School of Fine Arts in New York, as well as Art Center College of Design in Pasadena, California. Visit www.erikaoller.net.

THE END